To: Bobby the Blobby

This little book is
a little pick me
up .... hope you
like the philosophy

love you lots;
Nut
xx

LIFE Is a PIC-A-NIC

LIFE Is a PIC-A-NIC

YOGI BEAR'S
TIPS & TRICKS FOR THE SMARTER THAN THE AV-ER-AGE BEAR

by Yogi Bear with Earl Kress

INSIGHT EDITIONS

DEDICATIONS

I hereby dedicate this book to my little bear-type buddy, Boo Boo, and to the one true love of my life, *pic-a-nic* baskets!

—*Yogi*

This book is dedicated to the memory of my mentor, Daws Butler, the real voice of Yogi Bear. Also, to the memories of Bill Hanna and Joe Barbera, without whom there would have been a lot less joy in the world. And finally, to the memory of Doris Stanley, my mother-in-law—who, I believe, was even more excited about me writing this book than I was. When they invent the heavenly Kindle or iPad, I'm sure she'll be the first one reading the Afterlife Edition.

—*Earl*

CONTENTS

A Bear Without Care

When I was asked to collaborate on a book with Yogi Bear, I thought I was being given a great opportunity. Not only was I looking forward to spending time with a hero of mine, but I also figured it would just be fun to watch him in action. You know what they say, though: "Be careful what you wish for."

In some ways, Yogi is exactly as he seems, the happy-go-lucky bear without care. (The rhyming rubs off on you if you spend enough time with him.) But sometimes his one-track mind is a hindrance, because that single track is frequently not the one you want him on. Yogi is easily distracted, causing his train of thought to get derailed, often producing the equivalent of a five-car pile-up. What a mess!

Still, I have to thank Boo Boo, who, although he has no control over his big buddy's actions, is pretty good at steering him back on topic. I'd also like to thank Ranger John Smith of the National Park Service for his cooperation. The fact that he's been able to maintain his sanity is a testament to the man's fortitude.

(One other thing: As many of you know, Yogi has a very distinctive way of speaking. Therefore, to better convey the bear himself, I have taken the liberty of italicizing words Yogi has customized.)

Meeting one of your heroes is always dangerous, because you tend to start out with this idealized version of them in your head. It's very easy to become disillusioned and disappointed as you become familiar. I'm happy to say I've actually come away from this particular experience with greater respect for Yogi, and would even go so far as to say I consider him a friend. I hope he feels the same. If I give him a piece of chocolate cake, I'm sure he will.

—Earl

Life Is a Pic-A-Nic

Since this is the Introduction, allow me to introduce myself. I am a creature of the forest. And the particular forest I call home sweet home is Jellystone Park, where I live in a drafty old cave. I wear a hat and a collar and a necktie. "Why?" you ask. "Why not?" says I. In case you haven't unraveled this mystery, I am a bear who goes by the name of Yogi, and I do what I please.

I can sum up what makes me tick and tock in one word: *nonconformist*. I am a nonconformist bear, and I don't care. I don't act like the other animals. I don't dress like the other animals. And I certainly don't eat like the other animals. Instead, I choose to pursue *pic-a-nic* baskets, my *fav-o-rite* food.

> Someone once said, "Life is a *pic-a-nic*." That someone might have been me.

Which reminds me of a platitude with attitude. Someone once said, "Life is a *pic-a-nic*." That someone might have been me. Tee-hee-hee! Like the *pic-a-nic*, life is just there for the taking. But you have to grab

its opportunities when they are present, or someone else will gobble them all up and leave you nothing but crummy crumbs. And if you're clever, it'll sure be *de-lish-she-us*! A good *pic-a-nic* can do the trick double-quick. A tisket, a tasket, the *pic-a-nic* basket is full of what you put in it. And it'll all be there if you'll just take it.

Being happy is easy when you know how to grab hold of the *pic-a-nic* that is life and get away with it. My

way to get the goodies has been through being smarter than the *av-er-age*. And I'm willing to share with my fellow bear, so there!

In that sense, this book is a cookbook, so you don't get all shook. In these pages, I'll share what has allowed this bear to flourish through the ages—the tips and tricks I've used to distinguish myself in any situation (and then get out of it). In particular, it will tell you how to express yourself so that you, too, can come off sounding at least as smart as the smarter than the *av-er-age* bear. Follow my lead, and you'll be your own mastermind in no time.

I hope you will find a smidgen of smarts (and maybe a few yuks) in this little book. I wouldn't exactly call it a work of Art—more like, a work of Yogi. And that's probably the most work I'll ever do, eh, Boo Boo?

At this point, Yogi got up and left the room, probably in search of a pic-a-nic *basket. It seems that a lack of food to the stomach for Yogi is something like a lack of oxygen to the brain for most people. When he finally came back, I wanted to ask him to elaborate, but his mouth was full. So I thought it best just to let this one go. Now, on with the show—er, book.*

—Earl

THE ART OF CONVERSATION

or, How to Get Anyone to Do Anything

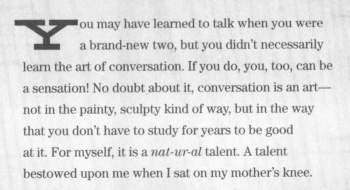

You may have learned to talk when you were a brand-new two, but you didn't necessarily learn the art of conversation. If you do, you, too, can be a sensation! No doubt about it, conversation is an art—not in the painty, sculpty kind of way, but in the way that you don't have to study for years to be good at it. For myself, it is a *nat-ur-al* talent. A talent bestowed upon me when I sat on my mother's knee.

She could talk a blue streak, or any other color of streak that struck her. This gift of gab has been like a personal savior. Sometimes, it gets me out of trouble, and sometimes it gets me in. But when it gets me in, I can always talk my way back out.

You can talk at people, or you can speak to them. The first is mundane and ordinary, while the second is dynamic and captivating.

I don't like to brag, but I am a sensational *con-ver-sa-tion-al-ist*. (Now that I think about it, I *do* like to brag! Ever since I was born, I've had to blow my own horn. Who who besides Boo Boo would do do it?) You can talk at people, or you can speak to them. The first is

mundane and ordinary, while the second is dynamic and captivating. And that's conversation. If you can learn the latter, it'll help you in the matter—the matter of getting goodies!

> *What could be worse than when you converse without some planning? It's important to use strategy.*

Now, let's think about this: What could be worse than when you converse without some planning? It's important to use *stragety*. Shooting off your big mouth can just blow up in your face. Think before you speak. And be forceful. You can't be meek when you're going to speak. Mumbling is for *bumblers*. It's just no good if you can't be heard or understood.

They say that talk is cheap. I don't know who *they* are, but they're oh, so wrong. Who makes more money than a talk show host? Some of said hosts may be cheap, but their words aren't. They get paid plenty to sit there and gab, gab, gab! And some of them can be pretty persuasive, like talking you into reading certain books. Salespeople are another breed of persuasive speakers. They get you to buy things you don't need and can't afford.

Before I wrap up this section, let me say, I *rezalize* that this book is somewhat slim, although it has some nice pictures of a certain *photo-genius* bear. That still doesn't give you the right to stand there in the book-store and read the whole thing. So, now that you've been caught red-faced and red-handed, I want you to buy not just the one in your hands but several copies— one to put away and keep in mint *con-di-tion* as a

> *They say that talk is cheap. I don't know who they are, but they're oh, so wrong.*

· ·

collector's item, and a few more to give away to other lovers of book-type writing. Do it for ol' Yogi!

There! That was your first lesson in how to get anyone to do anything. I not only taught you a thing or three, but I moved some product, too. There's only one thing I can say to sum this all up: I'm smarter than the *av-er-age* author!

PERSUASIVE REPERCUSSIONS

Here, now, I will give you some samples as examples of ways that I have talked, pleaded, and plain persuaded my way out of dicey situations. I will also explain how I wagged my tongue and sweet-talked, cajoled, and wheedled to make my prey do things my way.

"QUEEN BEE FOR A DAY"

. . . .

The ideal way to get someone to do what you want them to is to make them think it's their idea. For instance, one time Boo Boo said, "There's a colony of bees making honey in that tree." Then I said, "Boob, that's a great idea! You'll dress up as the Queen Bee to lure the bees away so I can get the honey!" Before you can say "Yellow Jacket Robinson," Boo Boo was in a bee costume, and he was sure he'd thought of the idea himself. At that point, I had to make sure that I *re-co-membered* to put aside some of the honey for my-own-self!

But as usual, he balked: "The Ranger isn't gonna like it." Then I convinced him that the Ranger wouldn't find out. And even if he did, there's no park rule against dressing

> *A lot of the art of persuasion has to do with your tone. I have confidence pouring out of every pore…*
> ·

in a costume. Still, he was uptight all night. So, I put his
mind at ease: "*Unlax*, Boo Boo, boy! Ol' Yogi has every-
thing under control!" A lot of the art of persuasion has
to do with your tone. I have confidence pouring out of
every pore, and what's more, I act like I know what I'm
talking about. Of course, when Boob got stuck in the
costume and chased by a crazed insect collector, then
I had to take my lumps, but at least I had a sweet treat
while I hit the street!

"PAPA YOGI"

· · · · · · · · · · · · · ·

The Father-and-Son Picnic was coming to Jellystone. How did I get the reluctant bear Boo Boo to do that voodoo that I do so well? I tempted his taste buds. Convinced him that it would require just a minor infraction to get in on the action. He wouldn't want to miss out on all those hot dogs, hamburgers, and delicious side dishes.

So, we found some tourist-type clothes hanging on a line and dressed up as Papa Yogi and his bear boy Boo Boo. There was no danger as long as we kept out of sight of the Ranger. But when we got caught, we found ourselves going who-knows-where on a bus with a bunch of fathers and sons who were sick, sick, sick from their overeating shtick!

"DO OR DIET"

. . . .

I always come out on top in any battle of words, no matter how long the discussion. That's why it was funny when Mr. Ranger and the Park Doctor tried to convince me that I was suffering from that bears-only illness, "*pic-a-nic-itis*." They said that if I took one more *pic-a-nic* basket, it was curtains for me. Not being one for frilly curtains, especially since my home sweet cave doesn't have any windows, I wasn't fooled for a minute. But Boo got worried, and he, too, said I should quit it!

Without any baskets, I lay in the road and caused a backup for miles, which made the tourists lose their smiles. The Ranger came running, and I went into my sad but incredibly persuasive tale, telling him it wasn't worth living without *pic-a-nic* baskets.

> *Sometimes, persuasion needs a little wordless boost. As they say, "Actions speak louder than words."*

Still, it didn't end. Sometimes, persuasion needs a little wordless boost. As they say, "Actions speak louder than words." *Per-son-al-ly*, I've never heard any actions speak, but I didn't let that stop me. I jumped off Lover's Leap, but the Ranger caught me with waiting arms.

Finally, as my *coop de grass*, I went into the ranger station on bended knee and used my patented Tearful Voice, begging for one final *pic-a-nic* basket, with which I would disappear into the hinterlands forever. Of course, I have no idea where the hinterlands are, but the Ranger had reached his breaking point and couldn't stand to see me suffer anymore. He handed me a basket loaded with goodies, some that I couldn't even pronounce, just as the Park Superintendent came in and caught him feeding a bear. The Ranger got his just desserts, while I just got dessert! *N'yay hay hee!*

SPICE UP
Your Speech

WHY I RHYME

. . . .

Why do I rhyme? That's like asking a canary why it keels over when it smells gas in a mine. Or like asking a mime to say something. Or like asking a tree why it won't leave. Or like asking Mr. Ranger if you can feed the bears.

Notice, if you will, that there wasn't a single rhyme that time. Oops! The bear can't help it!

But seriously, when it comes to rhymes, it's not like I try, guy! I'm just *nat-ur-al-ly* gifted. Rhyming keeps me pleasant in the present and grinnin' like I'm winnin'! It makes for a happy pappy and other stuff that'll sound too sappy!

You can't be sad or mad when your speech is peppered with snappy wordplay. When you think about it, words are like musical notes: You can put them together in infinite variations. Sometimes you get lyrics to a little tune from your arrangements, and sometimes you get something that would make Mozart or Madonna proud. (That's Sam Mozart and Harvey Madonna, who run the Snack Bar Deli at the park campground; their menu is full of rhymes.)

Either way, if you use a little pizzazz*, you can still communicate, but it's much more fun. Rhymes are like that. They can have "zazz" of their own. You can say the same old boring thing, or you give it a little swing and ring-a-ding-ding with rhymes!

. . . .
* *Notice that word has "pizza" in it? Lots more things should have pizza in it. Like my tummy, for instance. —Yogi*

NONSENSE WORDS

. . . .

"Ah, rooty-toot tooty, la ba da boo, gamma gimmee samma!"

Nonsense words are a crazy way to express yourself. They let you talk in rhythm without saying anything. It's not as popular as it was in the olden days, when this bear first came on the scene, but when it comes back, I'll be on the cutting edge.

Still, nonsense has something going for it. Nonsense talk can be all made-up words, or it can have some sense to its diction, even a combination of fact and fiction. For an instance, "Ah ba-zoo, ah ba-zing, and a big fat ah-ba-zoo to you, Boo Boo!"

The best part is, you can't do nonsense wrong. Just say whatever comes into your little head, Fred.

. . . .

Note that nonsense is replete with rhymes, which makes it doubly endearing. It can fill an awkward gap in a conversation, or you can use it when you're by yourself and strolling through the park one day. You might appear like you're cracking up by talking to yourself, but these days, half the tourists have gadgets in their ears that make it look like they're cracking up by talking to themselves anyway, so what's the diff?

The best part is, you can't do nonsense wrong. Just say whatever comes into your little head, Fred—give it a little rhythm, and you'll be on your way. Just like rhyming, it helps keep the grey away from your day!

WHAT CAN A CATCHPHRASE DO FOR YOU?
· · · · · · · · · · · · · ·

A great way to express yourself with some *in-dividu-al-ity* is to adopt a catchphrase or three. The catchphrase makes you memorable. When people hear it, they immediately think of you. Just make sure it's a good one. You don't want to be remembered for "I am not a crook" or "Boom goes the dynamite," or even "The Ranger isn't gonna like it, Yogi." (Sorry, Boob, you're still my bestest buddy, but it's time to retire that old bromide.)

A good catchphrase is all-purpose, like flour, only they're audible instead of edible. You can use them in a pinch, or when you get pinched. (In my case, it's usually by the Ranger.) Sometimes, you can employ your catchphrase when you don't know what else to say—sort of like nonsense words.

> *Sometimes, you can employ your catchphrase when you don't know what else to say.*

Other times, your catchphrase can act like punctuation, dividing up the parts of a conversation, so to speak. A good catchphrase can be used to start a conversation ("I'm *smarter than the av-er-age bear*." "It's true, your merits are many . . . "), end one ("How do we settle this?" "We do it my way, since I'm *smarter than the av-er-age bear*."), or diddle somewhere in the middle ("I'm

smarter than the av-er-age bear." "Huh, where did that come from?"). That's just how useful they are. They don't even know their place, nor do they need to. Get yourself a snappy catchphrase, and you can win friends and influence bears!

"SMARTER THAN THE AV-ER-AGE"
. . . .

My catchphrase, as if I have to tell you, is "I'm smarter than the *av-er-age* (*fill in the blank*)." By way of example, here is a sample: "I'm smarter than the *av-er-age* Ranger!" Or, "I'm smarter than the *av-er-age* tourist!" And, when it comes right down to it, "I'm smarter than the *av-er-age* bear!"

Why is this my catchphrase? *O-rig-in-al-ly*, I didn't intend for it to become a catchphrase. I was just stating the facts as I see 'em. But besides just stating facts, I suppose it has a lot to do with my bear-size ego. I could never think of myself as *av-er-age*; I'm not an *av-er-age* eater, sleeper, or thinker.

> *I could never think of myself as av-er-age; I'm not an av-er-age eater, sleeper, or thinker.*

The main advantage to this catchphrase is that no one else can use it. If the Ranger said it, you would fall on the ground and laugh yourself silly (which is not *necess-a-cess-arily* a bad thing—being silly can keep you from getting *illy**). The Ranger saying he's smarter

* *That may be my worst rhyme ever! —Yogi*

than the *av-er-age* anything makes no sense. They don't come any more *av-er-age* than Mr. Ranger. Don't get me wrong—some of my best friends are *av-er-age* (but they are definitely not rangers). I do not discriminate (that is, if I am not discriminated against).

And where can I use this oft-quoted *wordliness*? Anywhere I dare—that's where. There isn't a *sit-u-a-tion* that doesn't

lend itself to me declaring I'm better than it is. At least better than the *av-er-age sit-u-a-tion*, that is.

I test-drove a couple other catchphrases, like "What the
Ranger don't know won't hurt him" and "Smells like
somethin's burnin'," but they were just *av-er-age*. They
didn't roll off the tongue with the same lilting rhythm,
or have the *all-purposeness* of my smarter than the
av-er-age adage.

YOGANALYSIS: OTHER CARTOON CATCHPHRASES

. . . .

First of all, why did I call this section Yoganalysis? It makes it sound like my name is Yoga Bear. That's a whole different animal. Actually, he's still a bear, but he lives on the other side of the park, and he's much too calm for my taste. (And flexible—it's unnerving.) All that aside, I shall swallow my pride and get on with this.

Huckleberry Hound

Huck's number-one catchphrase is, "And a Huckleberry Ho-o-o-o-o-o-ound dog howdy, you all!" where he makes a howling sound, represented by those hyphened *o*'s. Being a hound-type dog, that makes sense, but as a catchphrase, it's kind of dense. He can use it only when he walks into a room. Imagine being in the middle of a conversation, and he starts "Howdying" all over you. It gets old pretty fast. I'd give this catchphrase 2 ½ green neckties out of 5.

"And a Huckleberry Ho-o-o-o-o-o-ound dog howdy, you all!"   + ½

Huck's other catchphrase isn't so much a catchphrase as it is a song. But since we've already talked about rhyming and rhythm, I'm going to allow it as a catchphrase, because he uses it so often. Huck's singing of the song "Clementine" is as much identified with him as his laconic demeanor. (I don't know what that means, but I've heard him say it before to describe himself.) Since Huck can't seem to remember the lyrics, including the titular what's-her-name as he sings it, he often dum-de-dums it. This so-called singing has more uses than his number-one catchphrase, but it's still not a very effective grabber. I'm rating this one 1 ¾ green neckties.

"Clementine" $+ \frac{3}{4}$

QUICK DRAW McGRAW

. . . .

Like Huck, Quick Draw has several catchphrases, but I'll begin with "Now, ho-o-o-o-o-o-old on thar!" or simply, "Hold on thar!" Note that in the first version, we once again have those hyphened *o*'s. (Those little guys sure get around the catchphrase circuit!) This catchphrase is *par-tic-u-lar-ly* useful because it's appropriate in a lot of situations. He can use it to physically stop, drop, and roll a bandit who's on the lam, or to verbally stop a wagging tongue.

Here's an example of the latter, which leads us to two more of the lawman's catchphrases: His sidekick, Baba Looey says, "But Queeksdraw, don' you thin'—," to which our horse-faced friend replies, "Now, ho-o-o-o-o-o-old on thar! *I'll* do the thinnin' around here! And *don't*

you for-get it!" Notice that he first interrupts Baba
Looey with the catchphrase we've been talking about,
and then he shuts down any further discussion of the
matter with the second, "*I'll* do the thinnin' (read:
thinking) around here!" There's also a variation on the
third and last one, which, by this point, as I'm sure you
can guess, is, "And do-o-o-o-o-on't you *for-get it!*" This
last one is a hoot and makes a statement with plenty of
emphasis, to boot!

I'm going to give Quick Draw's catchphrases a combined score of 3.14159265 green neckties. For some reason, I'm suddenly hungry for pie!

Quick Draw combined catchphrases × π

MR. JINKS

. . . .

This pussycat's catchphrase is, "I hate *meeces* to pieces!" This is all wrong on several levels. First of all, everyone knows that the plural of mouse is not *meeces* but *mouses*. So, what could you rhyme with *mouses*? "I hate *mouses* to houses?" "To spouses?" "To grouses?" None of those work.

Besides, it's a complete downer. Who wants to be around someone who's always repeatin' a phrase that promises a beatin'? Certainly not me or the *com-pan-y* that I see, nosiree! On the other paw, it's definitely unique. No one else could, or would, want to use it.

Overall, I think the nays drag it down to a score of ¼ green neckties, and maybe another ⅓ blue bowties.

SNAGGLEPUSS

Snaggdlepuss is a frustrated thespian, or a
hambone, as we say in the *ver-na-cu-lar*, so he
peppers his speech with theatrical terms like "gad-
zooks," "egad," and "forsooth." I would classify these
not as catchphrases, but as more like quirky bits of
dialogue. He does have another well-recollected and
oft-quoted catchphrase, though, that goes along with
his theatricality, and that is, "Exit, stage left!" or "Exit,
stage right!" depending on which direction his feet are
pointing. Like Huck's "Huckleberry Hound dog howdy,"
which can be used only on entering, Snag's line can be
used only when exiting, making it limited in its use.

Snag has the best catchphrase (besides mine, of course) of all time.

. . . .

However, his next catchphrase is a doozy. It's a variation on the tried-and-true, blast-from-the-distant-past
"Heavens to Betsy!" The pink lion's version, however,
is, "Heavens to Murgatroyd!" I have no idea who
Murgatroyd is, but then, I couldn't tell Betsy from a
park tourist, either. This catchphrase is especially useful when he's in a pickle or in the soup, but it can still
be used as simple punctuation.

Lastly, Snag has the best catchphrase (besides mine,
of course) of all time. It is so succinct, it goes beyond
being a catchphrase to being a catchword—that is, a

single word that's so effective, it can be used in any situation, and to fit any occasion. And that single word is "even." I know it doesn't look like much when you see it just sitting there, and I'm not trying to make excuses, but here are a few of it's uses: "Forsooth . . . fivesooth, even!" or "That's cruel, barbaric . . . Hanna-Barberic, even!" The simplicity of it is genius. I'm ashamed I didn't think of it myself. Still, I'm awarding it my highest honor: five green neckties, a collar with a string tie, and two cuffs.

"Even"

So, that's the good, the bad, and the Yogi. Hopefully, this Yoganalysis has given you enough stuff to create your own catchphrase— or at least suggested a few you might review.

Enjoy Your Goodies

Yogi thinks he doesn't follow the rules. But he does. They just happen to be his rules, rather than anybody else's.

And while Yogi's a bit of a bad bear in Ranger Smith's book, his bending of the park rules only really ends up impacting him most of the time. And sometimes Boo Boo. And almost always the poor, overwrought, and underpaid Ranger. And maybe a few tourists who end up lacking lunches. But that's a short list of victims when you consider the laughs and happiness he brings to the world.

Yogi's cheerful demeanor and happy outlook on life consistently make up for the few minor flaws in his character. Even his bombastic ego-driven catchphrase doesn't overshadow the overall delight one experiences when in his company. He is a bear among men.

During my time with him, Yogi shared a number of memorable thoughts, which I've tried to share in kind. I'll leave you, though, with one quote that I feel sums him up rather nicely, and I hope that it has similar meaning for you, too:

"Come what may at the end of each day, your pic-a-nic basket will be empty. But come the new day, when you go on your way, there will be another one chock full of goodies to enjoy! Oh, boy!"

May you enjoy all your goodies as much as Yogi does.

—*Earl*

I N S I G H T E D I T I O N S

10 Paul Dr.
San Rafael, CA 94903
www.insighteditions.com

Copyright © 2010 Hanna-Barbera.
™ & © Hanna-Barbera.
WB SHIELD: ™ & © Warner Bros. Entertainment Inc.
(s10)

PALA23511

Library of Congress Cataloging-in-Publication Data available.
ISBN: 978-1-60887-007-3

 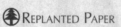

Insight Editions, in association with Roots of Peace, will plant two trees for each tree used in
the manufacturing of this book. Roots of Peace is an internationally renowned humanitarian
organization dedicated to eradicating land mines worldwide and converting war-torn lands into
productive farms and wildlife habitats. Together, we will plant two million fruit and nut trees
in Afghanistan and provide farmers there with the skills and support necessary for sustainable
land use.

Manufactured in India by Insight Editions
10 9 8 7 6 5 4 3 2 1

THANKS

Yogi and I couldn't have completed
this book without the help of
Denise Kress, Jerry Beck,
and Jake Gerli.

—*Earl*